The Mystery
~ of the ~
# Rescued Rubies

By Brad Strickland
Illustrated by Margaret Sanfilippo-Lindmark

CELEBRATION PRESS
Pearson Learning Group

Contents

Chapter 1
   Skipping Stones 3

Chapter 2
   What Is It? 12

Chapter 3
   Clues to the Past 19

Chapter 4
   Searching for Treasure 25

Chapter 5
   Deadly Tide 33

Chapter 6
   The Pirate King's Last Raid . . . 39

Chapter 7
   The Reward 45

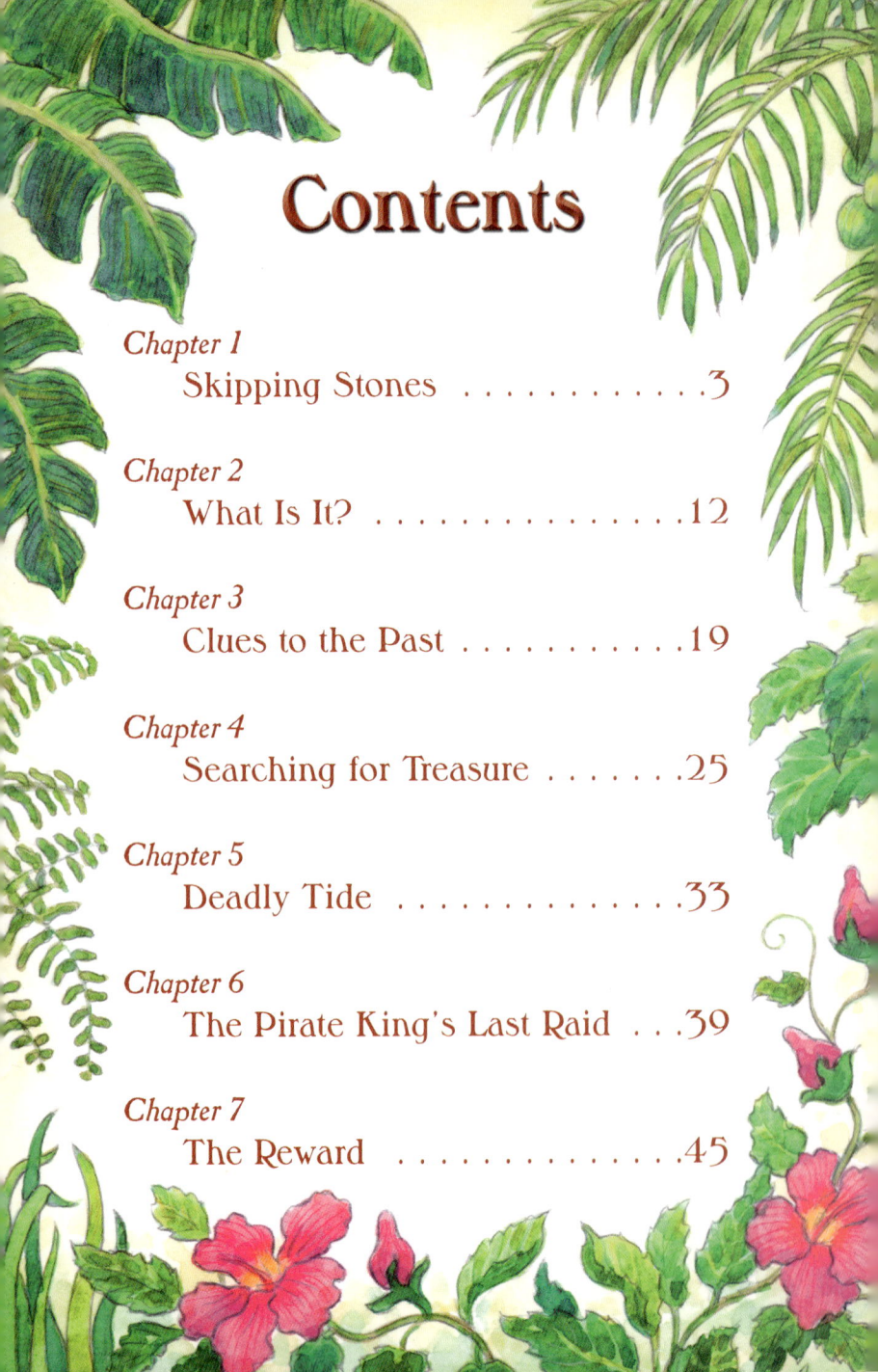

~ Chapter 1 ~
Skipping Stones

The rented automobile rode along a winding, shaded road. In the back seat, Marco Tomás and his younger sister, Cristina, tried to sit still and not ask, "Are we there yet?" That was difficult because this was their first visit to Puerto Rico. Their mother, Elena, had been born on the island, but she had come to New York to go to college, where she had met and married Marco and Cristina's dad, Philip Tomás.

Ever since Marco had been small, the Tomás family had been talking about taking a vacation in Puerto Rico to see their *abuelo* and *abuela*, Martin and Gloria Fernandez, instead of having their grandparents visit them. Now they finally were here!

Marco stared out the window at the junglelike landscape. "There are tigers out there," he warned Christina. "Maybe dinosaurs!"

Cristina laughed. "You're making that up."

Marco suddenly bounced up in his seat. "Look! I can see the ocean!"

3

They glimpsed sparkling blue water between the trees. "Maybe pirates are out there, waiting to attack," Marco warned.

"There aren't any pirates now," Mrs. Tomás said, "but there used to be, long ago."

Ahead, they saw a gleaming white beach. Cristina exclaimed, "We have the whole beach to ourselves!"

Their mom laughed. "That's one advantage of growing up here. I know the best picnic places."

As soon as everything was set up, Marco looked around. The beach rose in a gentle slope for a long way, then the land rose sharply to a stony cliff face. Here and there the tide had scooped out dark, mysterious openings that looked like caves. One was just a little way down the beach. Waves rolled right up into the opening.

Marco soon forgot about the cave as the family had fun wading in the ocean. After eating lunch, he looked around and said, "That's funny. The waves were all the way up to that cave, but now they stop on the beach."

"It was high tide when we arrived. Now it's almost low tide," Mr. Tomás explained.

"Can we explore the cave?" Marco asked with excitement in his voice.

"Yes, it's safe," answered Mrs. Tomás with a smile. "I used to check out these caves myself. Don't go in too far, though."

Marco and Cristina sprinted to the cave and peered inside. A pool had formed on the sandy bottom from water left behind by the tide. Marco waded in the lukewarm water, and in a moment, Cristina sloshed in to join him.

Marco looked around at the smooth boulders and the glistening cave walls, feeling a little disappointed that the cave wasn't deeper and more mysterious. Then he saw something odd—a rocky shelf, head-high, ran along one side of the cave. On it rested a small pyramid of what looked like white stones. Marco waded over to check it out.

"Look at this!" Marco said. He picked up one of the smooth stones. It was smaller than a tennis ball and slightly flattened. It felt strange in his hand, softer and heavier than a stone should feel.

"Hey, I wonder if I can make this stone skip." Marco brought his arm back, and with a quick snap, he threw the stone. It struck the surface of the pool, skipped twice, and sank.

"Let me try!" Cristina exclaimed. She picked up a slightly smaller stone and threw it. It hit once and sank.

"No, you have to move your arm sideways," Marco said, laughing. He threw another stone, this time getting three skips.

"Show me how," Cristina demanded.

Patiently, Marco instructed Cristina, demonstrating how to bring her arm back, snap it forward, and release the stone. Cristina threw two more before she was able to make one skip twice. "I did it," she announced with delight, "and I'm not going to stop until I can make one skip three times, like you."

"Three times is nothing," Marco responded. "Watch this, and you'll see a real expert at work."

He picked up a smaller stone and tossed it. The stone hit, skipped four times, then cracked hard against one of the boulders and bounced back to the sand. "It would be even better if we had really flat rocks. They skip better than these," Marco said.

"We could try some seashells," suggested Cristina, stirring up the sand on the bottom of the pool with one foot. "Lots of them are sort of flat, and we've got plenty to choose from here."

"These aren't heavy enough," Marco decided. "The other stones are better."

The shells were interesting, though, and Cristina began to construct a little pile of the better shells on top of one of the boulders near the cave entrance. "These will make good souvenirs," she told Marco.

Marco found something he thought was a shell, although it felt heavier than the seashells. It was black and shaped like an irregular circle. He tossed it on the pile because it seemed different from the other shells.

Mr. Tomás appeared in the cave opening and said, "The tide's coming back in, kids, so pack up. Your *abuelo* and *abuela* are expecting us for dinner, and we don't want to be late for that delicious Fernandez food."

Marco scooped up the three remaining stones as Cristina asked their father to help carry her pile of seashells back to where their mother waited. Mr. Tomás picked up the blackened circular piece that Marco had found and jiggled it in the palm of his hand curiously. "This isn't a shell. I think you may have found an extremely old coin here."

"It can't be a coin. It's black," said Marco.

"It might be," replied Mr. Tomás, "if it's badly tarnished. I'm not certain exactly what it really is, but it could be a *cruzado* or a *peso de ochos reales*—pieces of eight, that is. That's real pirate treasure!"

Mr. Tomás noticed that Marco had stopped to grab something from the water. Mr. Tomás asked, "What have you found now?"

It was the stone Marco had thrown that had hit the boulder on its last skip. He could see that it had cracked open, and something bright red gleamed from inside of it. The water had softened the "stone," and as Marco picked it up, the outside washed away. Marco stood staring down into the palm of his hand, his eyes wide in wonder. He was holding what appeared to be a gleaming red jewel!

~ Chapter 2 ~
What Is It?

"We found pirate treasure!" Marco exclaimed, leaping up and down on the beach near the cave. His mom hurried over, clapping one hand on her broad straw hat to keep it from blowing away in the gusty breeze. "Dad says we might have a coin, and now I've found a ruby or a red diamond or something!"

Mr. Tomás laughed as he held up the sparkling red gem that had come from inside the strange, round stone, turning it so that it flashed and glittered in the sun. "It's pretty, I'll admit that much," he said, smiling and shaking his head doubtfully. "Still, this is probably just an imitation jewel made of cut glass."

Mrs. Tomás took it and held it up to the light, tilting her head and watching the way the sun reflected off its surface. "Interesting, kids, but I think your dad may be right. This may be some kind of decoration from a ski boat that just happened to wash ashore, or maybe it's a spangle from someone's fancy bathing suit."

"Elena, *this* may actually be a genuine piece of pirate loot," Mr. Tomás said, showing her the blackened disk. "People could find a lot of treasure around here because back in the seventeenth and eighteenth centuries, many Spanish galleons wrecked off the coast. Bits of them probably are still washing ashore."

Mrs. Tomás handed the red jewel back to Marco. "I don't know about the coin, but I'll bet my cousin Osvaldo, who's a jeweler in San Juan, can tell you if this is a real ruby. I'm sure he'd look at it for you tomorrow."

"Why not today?" Marco groaned.

"We're having dinner with your grandparents," Mrs. Tomás said firmly. "They're really looking forward to it. Anyway, there's no reason to be in such a hurry! You'll still have the jewel tomorrow, and my cousin will still have his jewelry store. Now, everyone help me pack up."

The next morning, Mrs. Tomás took the children to her cousin's jewelry store. Marco felt just as excited as he had been when he first found the strange red stone.

Cousin Osvaldo was a cheerful man. He took them to his workroom. He perched on a stool and opened a drawer to find a jeweler's loupe, a magnifying eyepiece. Through the loupe, he stared at the red jewel, holding it under a bright white lamp. Then he whistled, sounding impressed.

"Congratulations," he said, smiling and shaking his head as if he still could not believe what he had seen. "What you have here is a very nice ruby with an amazing old-fashioned cut. I don't know if it's pirate treasure, but I'm sure it was mined and cut perhaps 300 years ago!"

"Cool! I knew it had to be real," Marco said with a triumphant grin of satisfaction.

"Can we keep it?" Cristina asked.

"There is a law about finding treasures such as this. Unfortunately, I am afraid you will have to report it to the authorities, and they may not allow you to keep it," Osvaldo said. "However, you will be paid a reward, although I couldn't guess how much."

Marco turned to his mom. "Is that true?"

"That's not fair," complained Cristina. "We found it, and what about all of the—"

Marco interrupted her quickly and said, "Will Cristina get to keep her seashells?"

Mrs. Tomás laughed, "Of course. Seashells don't have historical value. Osvaldo, how can we find out if this ruby is important?"

He replied, "I know a man who works for the Museum of Antiquities who might be able to help. Dr. Vargas knows a lot about artifacts like this. He's always busy, but I'll see if he'll speak with you."

As Osvaldo and their mom talked, Marco motioned for Cristina to follow him. They stood at the end of a glass counter, whispering.

"Why did you shush me?" Cristina asked.

"You were going to tell about the other stones we threw," he explained. "There were dozens of them. What if they had jewels in them, too? We'll have to convince Dad to take us back to the cave to find out for sure."

"Did you break open the ones you saved from the cave?" asked Cristina.

"No, and I'm not sure if we should."

Mrs. Tomás called to them. "Marco, Osvaldo has more good news for you."

17

Osvaldo held out a handkerchief, flourished it, and pulled out a shiny silver coin. "I think you can keep this," he said. "I've taken the tarnish off, and it looks as good as new, although it was minted way back in 1671."

"Whoa!" exclaimed Marco as he took the coin. Now that it was clean, he could see that on one side it had a cross dividing it into four parts. Between the arms of the cross were small images of a castle, some kind of animal, and two others too worn to make out. The other side had more markings, including some waves that might represent the ocean and some letters and numbers: *P8* and *PLV*, and a very faint B.

"It looks all wobbly," Cristina said.

"That's because it's a type of coin called a cob," Osvaldo explained. "*Cob* means 'a small lump of something.' Back in the old days, people who minted money would make a bar of silver, cut off little pieces, and hammer them into rough coin shapes. This is in good condition, and a coin collector might pay $100 for it."

18

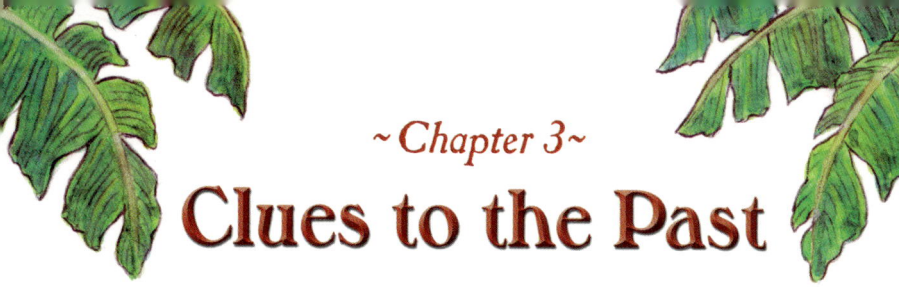

~Chapter 3~
Clues to the Past

In the car, Marco kept glancing at the old coin and imagining what else might be waiting for them in the cave. *It could be an enormous treasure*, he thought, *and if I can't keep it, at least I would be famous as the boy who had made this wonderful discovery.*

A little after noon, Osvaldo called with the news that he had arranged a meeting with Dr. Juan Vargas for that afternoon. Mr. Tomás said he wanted to come along, too. "Both Dr. Vargas and I are historians," he pointed out, "and the ruby should give us lots to discuss."

At the Museum of Antiquities, Marco's imagination took off as they went past displays. He wondered if real pirates had used the swords and worn the helmets. An attendant led them to an office and knocked on the door. A thin man with a pointed gray beard opened the door and said, "Come in. I can give you only a few minutes."

He doesn't sound especially encouraging, Marco thought.

19

Mr. Tomás introduced the family and said, "This is really my son's discovery, so I think he should tell you about it. Marco, go ahead."

Marco swallowed hard. Dr. Vargas was standing behind his desk with his arms crossed, frowning down at him. Stammering a little from nervousness, Marco described the cave and how he and Cristina had been exploring it when they found two exciting things. Marco showed Dr. Vargas the jewel and the coin.

Dr. Vargas sighed. "I know you would like me to tell you that you have found some splendid pirate treasure, perhaps even that you have found the loot of Fernando. However, the fact is that the sea washes up all sorts of things. The coin looks genuine, and I congratulate you on finding a memorable souvenir. As to the jewel, if it is a real ruby, you will have to report it to the government."

Mr. Tomás commented, "We know it's real. I'm surprised you're not more excited."

"Mr. Tomás," Dr. Vargas sighed doubtfully, "I assure you that at least twice a week some tourist comes to the museum filled with excitement and certain that he or she has discovered the treasure of Fernando, or some other pirate. Never has anyone found anything of real historical interest or value. I, myself, have explored all of the beaches and caves around here long ago."

"Who is Fernando?" Cristina asked.

"Fernando was a buccaneer, a pirate who plundered ships in the early part of the eighteenth century," Dr. Vargas said.

He turned and opened the door. "Legends say that before disappearing in 1702, Fernando fought with a British ship. Fernando's ship sank north of Puerto Rico and probably took him and his crew to the bottom of the sea."

"I can guess that the legend also says that Fernando escaped from his ship with a load of gold and jewels," remarked Mr. Tomás.

"You're absolutely right," replied Dr. Vargas. "It's all nonsense, of course, but that has not prevented people from seeking the treasure. If he had really escaped to hide his loot, surely someone would have discovered it long before now."

Dr. Vargas looked at his watch as if he wanted them to leave.

"Let's go," Mrs. Tomás said. "I'm sure Dr. Vargas has work to do."

"In a minute," Mr. Tomás said. "Dr. Vargas, how can we find out more about this pirate captain?"

Dr. Vargas said, "There's a display just down the hall." He handed Marco a brochure. "I'll see that you get the papers for reporting your find."

"Thank you for your time," Mrs. Tomás said, sounding a little stiff.

Out in the hall, Mr. Tomás said, "It's too bad Dr. Vargas wasn't more interested. At least we'll have fun looking at the display."

The display included a large map of the Caribbean showing islands where pirates had struck. Marco read the brochure that told the story of Fernando. Then he studied the picture of Fernando's pirate ship, *El Halcón*.

"Look, Cristina," Marco said, pointing to the picture. "It says *halcón* means 'hawk.'"

Cristina looked over his shoulder and asked, "Does it say anything about rubies?"

Marco replied, "No, but it says that Fernando captured ships in the Caribbean from 1697 to 1702 when *El Halcón* sank and Fernando disappeared. The British ship *The Huntress* searched for Fernando because he had taken a ship called *The Hope* that was carrying jewelry on its way to the queen of England."

"Then maybe Fernando did have rubies," Cristina said. "How did one get inside a rock?"

"I don't know," Marco confessed to Cristina, "but if the rock we found had a ruby in it, what about all the others? We've got to get back to that cave."

~Chapter 4~
Searching for Treasure

When they got back to their hotel room, Marco took one of the stones out of his suitcase and gave it to his dad. Marco explained how they had been skipping the stones and how one of them cracked open and had a ruby inside of it.

Mr. Tomás carefully looked at the white pebble. "I believe it's some kind of hard clay. Should we break it open to see if it has anything valuable inside it?"

Everyone wanted Mr. Tomás to break open the clay ball. He took it to the sink, softened it in hot water, and carefully rubbed at the clay. The white material dissolved quickly, and he held up another ruby, this one larger than the first. "Amazing!" he exclaimed.

"Dad," pleaded Cristina, "we've got to go back. Marco and I threw a lot of those things into the pool of water in the cave!"

Mrs. Tomás nodded. "We definitely should go back and sift through the sand on the floor of that cave. If nothing else, maybe we can prove to Dr. Vargas that tourists can find valuable things. We'll stop and buy some sieves so that we can really go through the sand. Let's go treasure hunting!"

After Mr. and Mrs. Tomás changed their clothes, the family all piled back into their rented car and drove along the twisting road again. If they were lucky, they would find more rubies in the cave. *What if the tide had washed them all out to sea?* wondered Marco. He felt terrible about throwing the stones into the pool, but how could he have known what was inside them? He daydreamed about how the rubies had gotten there in the first place.

The family arrived at the beach and hurriedly climbed out of the car. Dark clouds hung on the horizon. Waves, bigger than before, rolled in and crashed on the sand.

"There's a storm out at sea," Mrs. Tomás said, "and it's past low tide. We'll have to hurry."

They approached the cave and went inside. The waves were very close to the cave mouth, and they made a sound like thunder. Marco could not help shivering a little with anticipation.

Marco felt his heart drop a little as they all waded through the shallow pool inside the cave. No rubies glittered from the sandy bottom.

"Maybe they all washed away," Cristina said sadly.

"Where did you discover the pile of clay balls?" Mr. Tomás asked.

"Right over here," Marco said, sloshing over to the head-high stone shelf. "They were stacked up in a pyramid."

Mr. Tomás took a small flashlight from the pocket of his shorts and turned it on. "Hmm. It looks as if part of the cave wall washed away recently."

Marco could see that the place where he had found the clay balls did look as if blocks of the cave wall had crumbled, leaving behind the little shelf. Mr. Tomás shone the light on the stone. "Here's the solution to another mystery." He pointed at a brown, soggy layer of something. "This is decayed wood. I'll bet those clay balls were buried in a wooden box."

"A treasure chest?" Mrs. Tomás asked.

"Could be," Mr. Tomás replied. "Kids, where did you throw the stones?"

Cristina said, "We threw them toward the front of the cave. Most of them skipped, but some of my first ones didn't go very far."

"Then start sifting the sand from the bottom close by," Mr. Tomás told Cristina. "Marco, you go closer to the front of the cave and try your luck." Marco knelt in the water, scooped up some sand in his sieve, and swirled it around. He turned up only a few seashells. Behind him Cristina found something, but it wasn't a ruby. It was a corroded, rectangular frame of metal.

"It looks like a belt buckle," Mr. Tomás said, putting it in his pocket. "It may be a clue."

Marco scooped and swished. Just as he was beginning to think he would never find anything, two red jewels gleamed in his sieve. "I found some!" he yelled.

Mr. Tomás waded over to see. "Nice ones," he said. "Keep sifting."

Soon Marco discovered something round and solid. He grunted as he lifted it up. "What is this?" he asked, holding up a round, baseball-sized object made of corroded metal.

"That's a cannonball," Mr. Tomás informed Marco. He took the ball and placed it on the rocky shelf as Cristina called out that she had a ruby and some odd-looking metal.

The ruby was the largest one yet, and the pieces of metal were thin, looped, and swirled. Mr. Tomás inspected them. "I think these were made from gold plate," he said.

"That's gold?" Marco asked. The metal didn't look like gold. It was green and slimy.

Mr. Tomás rubbed at the metal with a handkerchief until it shone a bright gold.

Just then, Marco heard his mom call out with alarm, and a second later, he felt the push of a wave smack against his back. He gasped in surprise and spun around, seeing water flowing into the cave. Marco's family stood staring in horror as a big wave gushed right through the opening, roaring in so hard and heavy that Cristina lost her footing. Her mom grabbed her and held her tight just as another wave came sweeping up. The rising water had trapped them in the cave!

~Chapter 5~
Deadly Tide

"We're trapped!" Marco yelled.

His dad steadied him with a hand on his arm. "We stayed inside too long. With the storm out at sea, the high tide came in quicker than I thought it would," said Mr. Tomás. "Hang on! Turn your back to it!"

Another wave smashed into the cave and rolled right through, nearly pushing him over. The water in the cave was rapidly rising. At first, it had been ankle-deep, but now the water was up to Marco's waist.

"Stay close to the side and follow me," Mr. Tomás ordered. He waded toward the cave entrance, sticking close to the right wall of the cave. When the next wave hit, they all pressed against the wall to escape the force of the water. Now, it surged up to Marco's chest, even at the edge of the pool.

His dad was counting in an odd way: "One-Mississippi, two-Mississippi, three-Mississippi..."

"What are you doing?" Cristina yelled.

"He's counting seconds," Mrs. Tomás yelled.

Mr. Tomás shouted to Mrs. Tomás, "We have about seven seconds between waves. Elena, you take Cristina, and I'll get Marco. You go first and run as fast as you can off to the right, where the beach is higher. If these waves smash into you before you get to high ground, they'll pound you against the cliff. We'll go right after the next wave!" Mr. Tomás grabbed Marco's hand, and Marco didn't need to be told to hang on tight.

More water foamed in with the next wave. As soon as it began to pour out of the cave, Mrs. Tomás rushed out, staggering as the water tried to pull her legs from under her. Marco saw another big wave building up. Mr. Tomás was running, too. To Marco, everything happened in slow motion. He could see his mom desperately trying to get to the beach.

"Hold your breath!" Mr. Tomás ordered.

A huge wave towered over them, toppling them forward. Marco felt his father grab his arm. Suddenly, the water was pulling back, and Marco's head came out of the water.

His dad dragged him to his feet, and they ran up the beach before the next big wave could hit them. One crashed to the shore, but it was behind them now, and the foamy water that came surging in reached only to Marco's waist. Then he and his dad waded up out of the surf and onto the sand. Mrs. Tomás hugged her children, and they all turned to look at the cave. The tide was so high that only the very top of the opening showed above the waves.

"What about the stuff we found?" asked Cristina. "Did that all wash away?"

Mr. Tomás dug deep into his pocket and took out the belt buckle, the curved pieces of gold, and four rubies. "Let's hurry back to the hotel and change into dry clothes. Then I think we should pay another visit to Dr. Vargas."

Late that afternoon in Dr. Vargas's office, Mr. Tomás spread the rubies, gold strips, and belt buckle on the desk. "Pretty good for tourists, I'd say," he commented. Surprisingly, Dr. Vargas grinned.

To Marco's surprise, Dr. Vargas did not pick up the rubies first. Instead, he went straight for the belt buckle. He leaned forward, examining the metal as he looked at it under the lamp. Dr. Vargas looked up quickly and asked, "Where did you find this?"

Mrs. Tomás told him the name of the beach. "There's a cave on the west side. It's covered at high tide but above the water at low tide. That's where everything was."

Then Marco took one of the lumps of clay from his pocket. "The rubies were all inside these," he said. "I'm not sure what it is."

Dr. Vargas took it and scratched the clay. "It's a fine white clay that was rubbed into leather straps on navy uniforms to whiten them."

Then Dr. Vargas pulled out a huge book. "I owe you an apology," he said. He paged through the book until he found an old-fashioned engraving that showed a pirate holding a sword. Dr. Vargas tapped the belt buckle in the picture. "This is the only authentic portrait of Fernando, and I think he's wearing the buckle you found!"

The buckle in the picture was silver, with a skull and crossbones. Marco looked at the tarnished belt buckle on the desk and realized he could make out the same design.

~ Chapter 6 ~
The Pirate King's Last Raid

Dr. Vargas opened the book and began to tell the tale of Fernando the pirate. In the year 1702, England had a new ruler. Her name was Queen Anne, and even the English colonists in America wanted to celebrate Queen Anne's coronation. In Jamestown, Virginia, three talented silversmiths created a tiara, a delicate crown, studded with 37 fine rubies. The citizens of Virginia planned to send this fine present to Queen Anne in honor of her coronation.

Early in 1702, the tiara was taken aboard a merchant ship called *The Hope*, which sailed for England. To the ship's great misfortune, a week later, *The Hope* ran into *El Halcón*, Fernando's feared pirate vessel! Not a shot was fired. Knowing his ship could not stand up to *El Halcón*, the British captain surrendered and offered the tiara to Fernando if the pirate would let him and his crew go free.

Fernando agreed. Unfortunately for him, within a few days, the British ship crossed the path of *The Huntress*, commanded by Captain Anthony Burns. When Burns learned what Fernando had done, he vowed to track down the pirate and recover the jeweled tiara.

In his logbook, Captain Burns wrote, "The master of *The Hope* told us that Fernando had sailed south, and so we spread all the sails we could and followed her. On the seventh day, we spied Fernando's ship on the horizon."

Although *El Halcón* was a good ship, it was not as fast as *The Huntress*. The ships began firing cannons at each other while they were still far apart. Burns brought the Navy vessel alongside *El Halcón* while his gunners opened fire and pounded the pirate ship without mercy.

"I gave the order to board," Burns had written. "Our men swarmed aboard her, and after 30 minutes of fierce fighting, her crew surrendered. By then, *El Halcón* was sinking. We barely got our prisoners aboard *The Huntress* before the pirate ship settled to the bottom."

Burns questioned the surviving pirates. "Where is Fernando?" he demanded.

No one told him. Some just shrugged, while others said that Fernando had flown to the moon, and some said that he had chased a mermaid into the ocean. Burns was angry, but he could not solve the puzzle of what had become of the pirate king.

"One of our men swore that he had seen a small rowing boat pull away from *El Halcón*," Burns wrote. "We scoured the area but found no trace of any such boat. Could Fernando have escaped with his ill-gotten treasure? I do not know."

Dr. Vargas closed the book. "No more was heard or seen of Fernando, then or ever. He had just disappeared."

"He escaped, didn't he?" Marco asked. "He got away with the rubies, and we found them!"

"Possibly," Dr. Vargas said, smiling. "Let's imagine that Fernando had concealed the rubies from his crew by rolling them inside balls of clay and storing them in a box. When he and his men were close to Puerto Rico, Fernando slipped away in a little boat. His men didn't know where he had gone."

"Then he went into the cave to find a place to hide the box. He had to cut a hole into the rock to do that!" Marco exclaimed.

Mr. Tomás put a hand on Marco's shoulder. "That would take a long time to do," he said in a serious voice, "and if the high tide came rolling in...."

Marco gulped. He knew what had nearly happened to his family, and he could imagine the pirate turning from his newly hidden loot to discover that waves were rushing in, trapping him in the cave.

43

Dr. Vargas shrugged. "We cannot say for sure what happened. The belt buckle may mean that he drowned in the cave, or perhaps he changed clothes and left the cave disguised as a merchant or a farmer."

"I hope he didn't drown," Cristina said, "even if he *was* a pirate."

Dr. Vargas nodded solemnly. "He was an outlaw, but he must have been a brave and intelligent man, so we may hope he escaped. If he did, he obviously never returned to the cave because I think that you found his treasure."

"Do we get to keep these things?" Cristina wanted to know.

Dr. Vargas shook his head. "I'm afraid not. These are antiquities, and they will be given a home in the museum. However, you will probably get a reward for finding them."

"Could you put up a sign saying we found Fernando's treasure?" asked Marco.

"Maybe," Dr. Vargas said. "The first thing the museum will do is to send a team of archaeologists to that cave. There may be things there that even an intelligent group like yourselves may have missed!"

~ Chapter 7 ~
The Reward

School began soon after Marco and Cristina returned from Puerto Rico. They were so busy that they almost forgot about their adventure. Weeks later they were reminded when Mr. Tomás gave Marco a silver chain. Dangling from the chain was the silver coin Marco had found in the cave. Marco's friends were excited to see real pirate's treasure. Then, right before the winter holidays, Mr. and Mrs. Tomás announced, "Tomorrow we're flying back to Puerto Rico."

Mr. and Mrs. Tomás were mysterious about the trip. The family drove to the airport, boarded the plane, and flew to Puerto Rico with both Marco and Cristina asking question after question. Marco was ready to burst from curiosity by the time the plane landed.

As his family was walking through the airport, Marco saw familiar faces. Dr. Vargas and Cousin Osvaldo were waving to them and calling, "Over here!" Osvaldo took Mrs. Tomás's suitcase as Dr. Vargas led them out of the airport and toward a long, black limousine.

"Climb in!" Dr. Vargas said.

The limo stopped in front of the museum. A big sign said: "The Lost Treasures of a Pirate King: The Fernando Exhibition."

A huge grin spread across Marco's face. Inside the museum, display cabinets lined a wall. One had eleven rubies glittering on black velvet under a photograph of the cave. To one side was a life-sized sketch of Fernando with the belt buckle mounted on it, along with a scabbard and the hilt of a sword. On a shelf rested a five-foot-long model of *El Halcón*.

Best of all was a framed picture of Marco and Cristina, with a plaque under it describing how they had found the lost treasure of Fernando. Dr. Vargas gave Cristina a gold necklace with a small ruby. "This isn't one of the rubies you found, but I hope it will remind you of your great adventure," he said, smiling.

Then Dr. Vargas said, "Turn around and smile for the camera."

As the camera flashed, Marco was daydreaming. He was an archaeologist! He was an explorer. He would be famous some day....